HOW TO BE

A GOOD

MOTHER-IN-LAW

An Essential Guide To Being A Positive

And Supportive Mother-In-Law

DR. PATRICIA WALLER

Table of Contents

INTRODUCTION

Diana had always prided herself on being a good mother. She had raised her son, Alex, to be a respectful and responsible young man. When Alex got married to Rachel, Diana was overjoyed. She couldn't wait to welcome Rachel into the family and help her transition into married life. But things didn't quite go as planned.

Rachel was a strong-willed woman who had her own way of doing things. Diana, on the other hand, was set in her ways and had a hard time letting go of control. It didn't take long for conflicts to arise between the two women. Diana felt that Rachel wasn't respecting her authority as the matriarch of the family, while Rachel felt that Diana was trying to dictate her every move.

Their disagreements started small but soon grew into bigger issues. Rachel would often feel disrespected and belittled by Diana's comments and actions. Diana, in turn, felt that Rachel was being overly sensitive and not appreciating all that she was doing for her.

The tension between them was palpable, and it was starting to take a toll on everyone in the family. This story is typical of most Daughter-in-law and Mother-in-law relationship.

When your relationship with your daughter-in-law isn't cordial, you stand to lose lots of things, which includes closeness and companionship of your son, inability to share in the joys and successes of your son, you lose the opportunity to provide guidance and support to your son, you lose the chance to be involved in your grandchildren's lives, and to foster a relationship with them, you lose the privilege of being part of a larger family, you lose the respect and admiration from your daughter-in-law and family, you lose the chance to be invited to family gatherings, holidays, and other special events and lastly you lose the peace of mind of knowing that your son and daughter-in-law are getting along and happy.

Remember the old adage, ***"A son is a son until he takes a wife - but a daughter is a daughter all of her life"***. Why is that? Because a daughter will always remain close to her mother. Men grow up and find a new "mother" in their wife so to speak. Though you still have a place in their heart.

Understanding this makes you prepare by extending the same love and acceptance you have for your son to your daughter-in-law. This also reminds you that your daughter-in-law is now part of the family, and you should make an effort to build a relationship with her.

You should not forget that your daughter-in-law is still a daughter, and should be treated as such. You should welcome her into the family and make her feel as much a part of it as you son. You should also remember that a daughter-in-law has her own family and you should respect that. The truth is, **"if you treat your daughter-in-law as a daughter, you son will remain your son for life"**.

This old proverb is still used to describe the typical relationship between a mother and her daughter. While the adage is true in many circumstances, it is not always true in all cases. If a mother-in-law is a nice and supporting presence in the life of her daughter-in-law, the adage will not be accurate. The daughter will be close to her mother, but she also has a tight relationship with her mother-in-law.

A daughter can be close to both her mother and her mother-in-law, and both women can have a positive influence on her life. This book will guide you through how to prove this adage inaccurate because after reading and practicing the tips and advice in this book, you will be the best mother-in-law ever.

Follow me as I walk you through How to Become a Good Mother-in-law.

Check out my other books

How To Help Your Spouse Heal After Your Affair

Managing Conflicts In Relationship

CHAPTER 1

Understanding the Dynamic of the Mother-In-Law and Daughter-In-Law Relationship

The relationships between a mother-in-law and her daughter-in-law can be challenging and complicated, but it is critical to understand the dynamics involved in order to properly manage the relationship. On the one hand, it can be a loving, supportive, and affectionate relationship, on the other hand, it can be a relationship plagued with tension, conflict, and misunderstandings.

First and foremost, it is critical to acknowledge that the mother-in-law and daughter-in-law relationship is distinct in that it involves not just two people, but two families. This implies that numerous sets of expectations, values, and traditions must frequently be navigated and resolved. A mother-in-law, for example, may have different beliefs about how holidays should be celebrated or how children should be raised, which can lead to friction and stress.

Cultural and family history can have a considerable impact on the relationship between a mother-in-law and her daughter-in-law. For example, in certain cultures, a daughter-in-law is expected to pay reverence and respect to her mother-in-law, yet in others, they may be seen as equals. Family customs and expectations can also influence the relationship.

Both the mother-in-law's and daughter-in-law's personalities may have an effect on the relationship. They may get along faster if they have a lot in common, however different personalities might lead to conflict.

Communication is essential in every relationship, and this is especially true in the mother-in-law and daughter-in-law interaction. Miscommunication and upset emotions can occur when communication is not clear, honest, and courteous.

Boundaries have significance in any relationship, but particularly for the relationship between a mother-in-law and a daughter-in-law. Both the mother-in-law and the daughter-in-law may have opposing opinions about how much engagement in each other's life is suitable. A mother-in-law, for example, may desire to be extremely active in the life of her son and may be hurt if her daughter-in-law does not want her to be as involved as she would want. The daughter-in-law on the other side, may feel that her mother-in-law is being overly intrusive or domineering. To avoid disagreements and anger, both parties have to acknowledge and value each other's boundaries.

Expectations will have an effect on a relationship. For example, a mother-in-law may have certain expectations for her daughter-in-law while the daughter-in-law may have her own expectations for her role in the family. To minimize disappointment and animosity, it is critical to communicate and manage expectations.

Because both desire to be considered as the most important person in the family, competition is a natural dynamic in a mother-in-law and daughter-in-law relationship. The mother-in-law may believe she has a stronger claim on her son's attention, whilst the daughter-in-law may believe she is the main partner in the relationship. This competitiveness can present itself in both subtle and obvious ways, such as competing in cooking, housework, or childcare. It can also emerge as attempts to put on control over the relationship, such as dictating the conditions of visits or vacations.

One of the hurdles of the mother-in-law relationship is that it is frequently molded by social norms and stereotypes. For example, it is often regarded that mothers-in-law are tough and interfering, but daughters-in-law are viewed as ungrateful and demanding. These misconceptions can cause stress and misunderstandings between the two parties, making it difficult to establish a productive relationship.

So, how do you cope with the complex dynamics of the mother-in-law relationship?

Tips To Cope with the Complex Dynamic of the Mother-in-law Relationship:

Communicate Openly and Honestly: Communication that is open and honest is one of the best strategies to avoid conflict and misunderstandings. This includes being open to hearing each other's points of view and being prepared to compromise when required.

Establish Boundaries: It is critical to draw clear lines between what is and is not acceptable in terms of engagement in each other's lives. This can aid in the prevention of misunderstandings and conflict.

Avoid Competing: Try not to compete with your daughter-in-law. Instead, concentrate on developing a constructive relationship based on mutual respect and understanding.

Dispel Stereotypes: Be free to question preconceptions and cultural expectations around the mother-in-law relationship. Recognize that each person is unique and that the relationship cannot be approached in a one-size-fits-all manner.

Seek Professional Help: Consider obtaining professional help from a therapist or counselor if you are having difficulty navigating the mother-in-law relationship. They can provide you the tools and methods you need to have a good connection with your daughter-in-law.

Roles of A mother-in-law

The role of a mother-in-law varies widely across cultures and families. In general, a mother-in-law can play a significant role in the dynamics of a family. Here are some of the possible roles a mother-in-law can play:

Support: A mother-in-law provides her son and daughter-in-law emotional and practical support. This assistance can take numerous forms, such as providing childcare, assisting with domestic duties, or providing counsel and direction.

Mediator: In certain households, a mother-in-law can act as a mediator between her son and daughter-in-law. She can give an impartial viewpoint and assist in issue solving.

Mentoring: A mother-in-law can mentor her son and daughter-in-law. She can share her life experiences, provide wisdom and advise, and assist them in overcoming obstacles.

Grandparent: A mother-in-law can have a significant impact on her grandchildren's life. She can provide love, care, and attention, as well as contribute to the creation of unforgettable memories.

Friendship: A mother-in-law can develop deep friendships with her son and daughter-in-law This form of relationship is built on mutual respect, trust, and affection and will bring a lot of joy and happiness.

Important of Being a Good Mother-in-law

Being a good mother-in-law is crucial because it can have enormous impact on your daughter-in-law happiness and well-being, as well as your own family dynamics. Below are some of the benefits of being a good mother-in-law:

It creates Stronger Family Bond: A good mother-in-law takes the time to get to know her daughter-in-law and cultivates a pleasant connection with her. This will aid in the creation of a pleasant family atmosphere and the strengthening of family bonds. When you make an effort to get to know your daughter-in-law and show interest in her life, it will lead to a stronger and more meaningful relationship between the two of you. This will enrich your own life and bring new joy and fulfillment to your family relationships.

It aids in the avoidance of disputes and misunderstandings: A good mother-in-law talks with her daughter-in-law freely and politely, which helps to avoid misunderstandings and problems. This will result in a more harmonious and beneficial family dynamic.

It provides a positive example for future generations: When you model positive behavior and treat your daughter-in-law with love and respect, it sets a good example for your children and grandchildren to follow. This can help to create a family culture that values kindness, understanding, and empathy. When your children become parents, they are more likely to emulate you if you are courteous, friendly, and supportive.

It improves your happiness and well-being: A healthy relationship with your daughter-in-law will provide additional joy and happiness to your life. You may discover a new friend and ally in your family, which will improve your life in a variety of ways.

It enhances your own personal growth: Being a good mother-in-law can challenge you to develop new skills and attitudes, such as communication, empathy, and conflict resolution. This can help you to grow as a person and become a better listener and communicator.

Being a good mother-in-law is crucial not only for your daughter-in-law and family's well-being, but also for your own personal growth and development.

CHAPTER 2

Strategies for Building Positive Relationship with your Daughter-in-law

Building a strong relationship with your daughter-in-law can be a beautiful and rewarding experience that enhances both of your lives and deepens family ties. It takes work, understanding, and open communication, just like any other relationship. In this chapter, I will look at some ways for cultivating a pleasant and harmonious relationship with your daughter-in-law. You will be able to create a supportive environment that fosters trust, respect, and love by applying these strategies, thereby laying the groundwork for a long-lasting and meaningful relationship. Remember that every relationship is different, so tailor these strategies to your individual situation and enjoy the adventure of developing a strong friendship with your daughter-in-law.

Set Boundaries and Respect them

In a mother-in-law daughter-in-law relationship, establishing and maintaining boundaries is critical for both sides to feel appreciated and heard. First and foremost, it is critical to set each person's boundaries and expectations for the relationship. This may be accomplished by engaging in an open discussion about what each individual expects from the other. Once the expectations are set, it is critical to respect and honor them. This implies that you both should endeavor not to violate any established boundaries and should be conscious of each other's feelings when engaging in talks or activities. Furthermore, keep in mind that boundaries can change over time, and both of you should be willing to modify them if necessary. It is important to remember that both of you should be willing to compromise and work together to create a healthy relationship.

Take Time to Get to Know Her Interests and Hobbies

Having a daughter-in-law is a unique relationship that has its own unique challenges. Getting to know your daughter-in-law's interests and hobbies is one of the finest way to create a good bond with her. Talking to your daughter-in-law and seeing her behavior are the greatest ways to learn about her interests and hobbies. Discover what she enjoys doing in her spare time, what books she enjoys reading, and what topics she enjoys discussing. Encourage her to try new things and explore her interests, and be interested in the things she chooses to do.

Tips To Assist You Learn About Your Daughter-In-Law's Interests:

1. **Ask her questions:** Ask your daughter-in-law questions about her hobbies and interests to demonstrate genuine interest in her. Find out what kinds of music she loves, books she likes to read, movies she likes, and so on.

2. **Take her out**: Plan a pleasant day for your daughter-in-law. Take the opportunity to spend quality time with her

and get to know her better, whether it's a day of shopping, a movie, or a day at the zoo.

3. **Offer to assist:** If your daughter-in-law has a passion or a project she's working on, offer to assist her. Demonstrate your interest in her hobbies and willingness to assist her.

4. **Purchase a present for her:** Show your daughter-in-law that you care about her by purchasing a gift that is linked to her hobbies or interests. A thoughtful present, whether it's a book or a work of art, will convey your affection for your daughter-in-law.

Spend Quality Time Together

Invite her to join you for meals, plays, or other activities that you all enjoy. One of the way you can know your daughter-in-law better is by spending time together.

Tips For Spending Time Together:

1. *Establish a regular date night:* Make a regular date night with your daughter-in-law a tradition. A monthly dinner or lunch date, or even a weekly coffee or tea date, may suffice. This will not only allow you to get to know

each other better, but it will also demonstrate to her that you care about her and want to make time for her.

2. *Take her shopping:* Make a day of it by going shopping with her. This is a great way to spend quality time together while also giving her the opportunity to choose something unique for herself.

3. *Plan a special activity:* Spend an afternoon together doing something special. This may include going to the cinema or a museum, as well as taking a culinary lesson or going on a nature walk. The idea is to arrange something that both of you will like.

4. *Take a stroll:* Sometimes the greatest way to spend quality time with someone is to simply go for a walk. This is an excellent opportunity to catch up on each other's lives and discuss anything is on your mind.

5. *Host a game night*: Host a game night with your daughter-in-law and other family members. This will make her feel included and will allow you to bond over some friendly competition.

6. *Have a picnic*: Pack a picnic and travel to the park for an afternoon of relaxation. This is an excellent opportunity to catch some fresh air and spend quality time together.

7. *Invite her over for dinner*: Demonstrate to your daughter-in-law that she is welcome in your home by inviting her over for dinner. This is an excellent strategy to get to know each other better and prove to her that she is also a member of the family.

Listen To Her

Really listen to what she has to say and avoid giving unsolicited advice.

- ★ Listen to her with an open mind and no preconceptions. Tell her she can talk to you freely and honestly without fear of being judged.
- ★ In order to encourage her to clarify her ideas and feelings, ask her questions. Demonstrate an interest in understanding her point of view.
- ★ Recognize her Feelings without attempting to solve the situation. Tell her you hear her and that her feelings are genuine.

★ Provide emotional support and understanding. Tell her you're here for her and that you care about her.

★ Even if you disagree with her judgments, respect them. It is critical to demonstrate to her that you respect her autonomy and will not impose your decisions on her.

★ Give her space to deal with her issues on her own. It's always best to let her figure out her solutions without interference.

Show your Appreciation for Her Efforts.

Appreciating your daughter-in-law is an important strategy to build your relationship with her.

***Thank her with wonderful words*-** Take the time to commend her on her accomplishments, parenting, or simply how she is. Express your heartfelt gratitude and let her know how much you value her. Take action to express your thanks. Offer to assist with domestic tasks, run errands, or babysit. Show your gratitude with a meaningful present, such as a flower bouquet or a treasured piece of jewelry.

Avoid criticism - Don't criticize her decisions or actions. Instead, offer constructive criticism if needed. Criticism will always lead to defensiveness, which can quickly escalate into arguments. Remember that your daughter-in-law is an essential component of your family and deserves to be treated with dignity. If criticism is not handled in a respectful and constructive way, it can damage the trust between you and your daughter-in-law, and can lead to serious conflicts.

Constructive Criticism focuses on your *feelings*, the *behavior* (of your daughter-in-law) not on the person (your daughter-in-law)

Don't Say: "You always do this!" **Say**: "I feel frustrated when ...", **Don't say**: "You don't respect me "**Say**": It hurts me when..."

Even if you disagree with her ideas or thoughts, remember that criticizing her is not the best method to settle any problems that may emerge. Instead, strive to communicate and discuss any disagreements in a nonjudgmental, open, and courteous manner. Respect her right to her own thoughts and points of view, but still remaining open to compromise and understanding. If discussion fails to resolve an issue, it is often appropriate to simply agree to disagree and move on.

Make Sure to Communicate With your Daughter-in-law on a Regular Basis

Communicating with your daughter-in-law on a regular basis is important for a number of reasons. First, it allows you to stay connected and build a strong relationship with her. This help foster a positive relationship between the two of you and create a supportive environment for your son. Additionally, regular communication can help you stay up to date with the latest news in your son's and daughter-in-law's lives, including any major changes or milestones. This can help you be better prepared to lend a hand if help is needed. Finally, communication with your daughter-in-law is a great way to create a bond and show her that you care about her and her family.

CHAPTER 3

How To Be A Good Mother-In-Law

While being a mother-in-law can be an uphill task, it can also be extremely rewarding. After all, your son has picked the lady with whom he will spend the rest of his life, and it is critical that she feels welcomed and accepted into your family. Anyone can learn to be a wonderful mother-in-law with time and effort.

Here are some guides to help you become a loving and supportive Mother-in-law

Respect your Daughter-in-law's Decisions.

Respecting your daughter-in-law's decisions demonstrates to her that you appreciate her viewpoint and trust her judgment. Accepting a different point of view from someone who is not family but has become part of your family can be challenging. Respecting your daughter-in-law's decisions proves that you recognize her perspective and regard her as an individual. This can enable you and your daughter-in-law develop a strong and healthy connection, which will benefit your entire family. It can also assist to build your relationship with your son, as he will appreciate that you are considering his wife's point of view. It also sets a good example for your son, as he will learn to respect his wife's decisions as well.

Avoid Giving Unsolicited Advice, and be Open-minded to their Parenting Style.

One of the greatest ways to avoid unsolicited advice and questions concerning your daughter-in-law's parenting style is to stand aside and allow her decide how she wants to raise her children. Respect her right to make decisions for her children that she believes are best for them . Show your daughter-in-law that you are willing to assist her in any manner she may require. Demonstrate an interest in her parenting decisions and an openness to hearing her thoughts. Be readily accessible to assists out with childcare when needed, but don't overstep your boundaries. Respect the fact that your daughter-in-law is the primary caregiver for her children and understands what is best for them. Offer your assistance when requested, but do not push your thoughts or opinions on her. Be courteous and supportive of any decisions she takes.

Furthermore, try to focus on developing a solid relationship with your daughter-in-law and expressing your gratitude for the excellent elements of her parenting. This will contribute to an atmosphere of mutual trust and respect between you. Provide compassion and support to your daughter-in-law. Demonstrate to her that you are available to her when she needs to chat or seeks guidance. Let her know she can come to you for assistance and that you are available to listen and understand.

Treat Her With Kindness and Show Appreciation for Her Efforts.

Make a point of thanking her for her presence in your family and the great influence she has. Provide specific compliments and acknowledgements for her efforts, such as her care for your son, home contributions, or development of family bonds.

Show real interest in her feelings, experiences, and well-being by being attentive and sympathetic. When she discusses her opinions, problems, or accomplishments, be a caring listener. Validate her feelings and offer assistance when she requires it.

To express your thanks, consider drafting a handwritten note or emailing a thoughtful message. Write about the specific things she has done that you admire and how they have benefited your family or life. This particular touch has the potential to make her feel wonderfully treasured.

Show your gratitude via your deeds. Consider performing tiny acts of kindness, such as preparing her favorite meal, volunteering to assist with home tasks, or surprise her with a modest present.

Be enthusiastic about her accomplishments, huge and little. Recognize and appreciate her accomplishments, whether they are professional, personal, or a new talent she has learned, to increase her confidence and sense of belonging.

Pay close attention to her emotional well-being. Provide a sympathetic ear and support her feelings without ignoring or dismissing them. Demonstrate empathy and compassion, and let her know you care about her pleasure and general well-being.

Offer Help and Support when Needed

Rather than making assumptions, ask her directly how you can assist. By requesting her feedback, you demonstrate respect for her freedom of choice and understand that her needs may change depending on the scenario.

Providing emotional support and being a good listener can be really beneficial most times. Be present and attentive when she needs to discuss or let go her frustrations. Empathy, understanding, and encouragement are all appropriate responses. Avoid giving her unwanted advise until she directly requests it.

Offer practical assistance with chores that will reduce her workload. This might range from grocery shopping to making a meal to aiding with housekeeping. Consider her individual requirements and provide aid accordingly.

Recognize that her wants and tastes may vary over time and be flexible and accommodating. Be flexible and open to change your assistance as needed. When giving assistance, demonstrate your willingness to work around her schedule or preferences.

It is critical to respect her boundaries while providing support. Recognize that she may prefer to do certain chores alone or may have specific preferences for the sort of assistance she requires. Respect her judgments and offer aid within the parameters she establishes.

Approach things with empathy and patience. Avoid offering judgment or criticism, and reassure her that you are there to help her without passing judgment. Be patient if she need time to accept or request help.

Respect their Privacy and Don't Overstep Boundaries.

Maintaining a healthy relationship requires you to respect your daughter-in-law's privacy. It is essential to keep in mind that although you are family, your daughter-in-law is her own person and has a right to her own boundaries and privacy.

The first step in protecting your daughter-in-law's privacy is to be cautious about the information you reveal about her.

It is not your job to reveal personal information about your daughter-in-law unless she expressly consents. This includes information about her relationship with your son, her job and career, her financial situation, her health, and any other sensitive topics. Furthermore, it is critical not to gossip about your daughter-in-law or disclose information that could harm her reputation.

You should also respect your daughter-in-law's physical space. Respect her boundaries by not entering her room or residence without her permission. Do not take her food or stuff without first asking permission. Also, in chats, respect her right to privacy. Do not listen in or interrupt her interactions with your son or other family members.

It is also critical to offer your daughter-in-law the freedom to make her own decisions. Try not to exert control over her or her connection with your son. Respect her right to make her own choices and judgments, and avoid expressing your opinion or advise unless she expressly requests it. Additionally, it is important to respect her right to say **"no"** to any requests or invitations, and not to take it personally.

Finally, it is important to be conscious of your own behavior. Be mindful of how your words and actions may be perceived by your daughter-in-law, and ensure that your conduct is respectful and suitable. Make no criticisms or derogatory remarks about her. Instead, concentrate on developing a nice relationship with your daughter-in-law and demonstrating that you care about her.

Celebrate Special Occasions and Family Events.

Celebrating key holidays and family gatherings is a great way for a mother-in-law and her daughter-in-law to build their friendship. It helps you to get to know one another in a relaxed and pleasurable setting. Birthdays, holidays, anniversaries, and other major anniversaries can help to develop a sense of community and appreciation for one another. It also allows you to share your stories and experiences, which can help build trust. Furthermore, family gatherings like reunions, picnics, and other get-togethers can be a great way to bring the family together and strengthen the bond between mother-in-law and daughter-in-law.

Celebrating special occasions and family events with your daughter-in-law can be a great way to show her that you care about her and appreciate her as part of the family. It can be as simple as taking her out for a special dinner or surprise her with a gift. Showing up to family events, such as graduations, birthday parties, and baby showers, is another way to show your daughter-in-law that she is part of the family. It can also be a great way to build a strong bond between the two of you. Additionally, it can help create a sense of belonging and support for your daughter-in-law. Finally, it can be a great way to show your son that you respect and value his wife.

Refrain From Making Negative Comments About Her Family or Friends.

You guarantee that your daughter-in-law and her family feel appreciated and welcomed by avoiding unpleasant comments, which is the cornerstone of a strong relationship. Furthermore, unpleasant comments might sour the relationship between you and your daughter-in-law and her family.

As a result, it is critical to be mindful of what you say and to express yourself in a courteous and constructive manner. It is also important to ensure that your statements are not misinterpreted or taken out of context. If you disagree, try to keep your attention on the subject rather than on personal assaults or criticism.

Stay in Touch and Maintain Regular Contact.

It is essential to have frequent communication with your daughter-in-law for a variety of reasons. It will assist develop and deepen family bonds, give support and advice, and improve the entire relationship. Regular communication will also allow you to get to know her better and create a more open and honest connection. Furthermore, in order to keep connected with your daughter-in-law and her family, it is essential to have regular communication with her. This is especially important if your son and daughter-in-law reside a distance away or have their own children. Maintaining contact can assist your son, daughter-in-law's and grandkids feel connected to their extended family.

Respect Their Authority When it Comes to Disciplining Their Children.

When it comes to setting limits and disciplining, a mother-in-law should respect her son and daughter-in-law's authority by recognizing and respecting their preferences. She should provide advice, but ultimately respect their judgments and refrain from imposing her own.

A mother-in-law can express her affection for her grandchildren and be an active participant in their life without encroaching on the authority of her son and daughter-in-law. She can enhance her relationship with her grandkids while still respecting her son and daughter-in-law's parenting approach. Finally, a mother-in-law may provide support, comfort, and counsel tailored to her son's and daughter-in-law's family beliefs and parenting objectives.

When it comes to discipline, a mother-in-law should provide her support and advise when requested, but she should accept her son and daughter-in-law's decisions. A mother-in-law should constantly remember that her son and daughter-in-law are in charge and in the best position to determine the most successful parenting practices for their children.

In addition, you should also take care not to undermine the authority of your son and daughter-in-law by engaging in arguments with them or making comments that may come across as critical.

CHAPTER 4

Managing Conflict Through Effective Communication

Conflict is an inevitable part of any relationship, there will always be moments of disagreement in a mother-in-law and daughter-in-law relationship. Managing conflict through effective communication is a essential skill for building successful relationships and attaining goals. Effective communication will aid in the reduction of unpleasant emotions, the promotion of understanding, and the establishment of trust. It will also aid in the identification of underlying issues and the development of a healthy discussion that leads to mutually beneficial remedies. Both of you can get a greater knowledge of each other, achieve a consensus, and move on in a positive path by employing effective communication.

Avoid Bringing up the Past

Bringing up the past during conflict resolution can be damaging because it can lead to a deeper level of hurt and resentment, and it can also inflame the situation. It can also lead to a rehashing of old grievances and hurt feelings, which can be difficult to reconcile. Additionally, revisiting the past will prevent the you and your daughter-in-law from looking to the future and finding a constructive solution. It's important to focus on the current issue and the future, rather bringing up the past, in order to find a positive resolution.

Listen to Your Daughter-in-law

One way to listen to your daughter-in-law is to practice active listening. This means making eye contact, not interrupting, and displaying nonverbal cues such as nodding and smiling to show that you are listening and understanding. It is also important to avoid distractions such as checking your phone or replaying conversations in your head. Allow your daughter-in-law to finish her thought before responding and be sure to ask clarifying questions if you are confused. Additionally, it is important to focus on the content of the conversation and not trying to jump to conclusions or offer advice. Finally, it is helpful to summarize what your daughter-in-law has said and to ask if you have correctly understood their point of view.

Respond to Criticism With Empathy

Stay calm and don't become defensive. Acknowledge your daughter-in-law's point of view, thank her for bringing her concerns to your attention, and validate her feelings. Try to focus on understanding your daughter-in-law perspective rather than defending your own. Ask questions to gain a better understanding of her feelings and views, and offer constructive solutions to help resolve the conflict. Let your daughter-in-law know that you understand how she feel, and why she feel that way.

Admit When You are Wrong

To effectively admit that you are wrong during a conflict resolution, start by being honest and open about your mistake. Acknowledge that you made a mistake and take ownership of it. It is also important to explain why you think you made the wrong decision and how you plan to avoid making the same mistake in the future. Apologize for any hurt or harm caused and make sure to take responsibility for it. Show your willingness to make things right and ask for forgiveness. Finally, be open to your daughter-in-law ideas and suggestions for how to move forward. If appropriate, make a plan of action to ensure that the mistake does not happen again.

Take a Time Out

Conflict resolution is a process that requires patience and understanding. Taking time out during the process can be very beneficial in helping you both step back and reflect on the situation in a more productive manner. Time-outs allow for a break in the intensity of the moment and can help clear the air, allowing you and your daughter-in-law to cool off and think more clearly. Additionally, it gives you and your daughter-in-law time to re-evaluate the situation, and consider options for a resolution that may not have been considered before. Taking time out during conflict resolution can help you to better recognize and understand your own emotions, as well as those of your daughter-in-law. It can also provide a space for you both to come up with creative solutions, and access what has been said in order to move the conversation forward.

CHAPTER 5

How To Prevent Future Conflicts

Though conflicts are inevitable in relationships, they can be prevented from happening in the future. Below are strategies to prevent future conflicts.

Creating an Atmosphere of Respect and Understanding

Creating an atmosphere of respect and understanding is essential to preventing future conflicts in relationships.

To create an atmosphere of respect and understanding, it is important to practice active listening. This means actively engaging in conversations, showing respect for the other person's point of view, and responding thoughtfully. It also involves practicing empathy and compassion. This will help create a safe and secure environment where you and your daughter-in-law can express yourselves without fear of repercussions.

It is also important to practice effective communication skills such as assertiveness, honesty, and being nonjudgmental. Focus on resolving conflicts in a healthy and productive manner. Instead of resorting to arguments or criticism. Ask questions and try to come up with solutions that work for both of you. Set boundaries and respect them. Make sure both parties are clear on what is and isn't acceptable behavior. Learn more about Effective Communication here.

Practice Effective Communication

Effective communication is an important tool in preventing future conflicts in relationships. When you and your daughter-in-law understand each other's needs, wants, and expectations, you can better avoid potential areas of disagreement.

Effective communication allows you and your daughter-in-law to express your thoughts and feelings without fear of judgment or criticism. This helps to ensure that both of you feel heard and understood.

It also encourages you to consider your daughter-in-law's perspective and to discuss issues before they become a source of conflict. In addition, effective communication promotes respect, trust, and empathy. When these qualities are present in a relationship, it is much easier for both parties to work together.

Finally, effective communication allows both of you to work together to find creative solutions to problems. By working together, both of you can brainstorm ideas and develop strategies to resolve conflicts that are mutually beneficial. This helps to ensure that you both are satisfied with the results and that future conflict can be avoided.

Apologize When you Should

Apologizing is an important part of any relationship, and it is a great way to prevent future conflicts. When you takes responsibility for your actions and apologizes, it will help to create an atmosphere of mutual understanding and respect. It will also help to foster a sense of trust and openness between both of you. Apologizing shows a willingness to take responsibility for one's mistakes and to try to fix them. This will help to prevent future conflict by ensuring that both of you view each other as trustworthy and willing to work together to resolve any issues. Additionally, apologizing can help to reduce feelings of resentment and bitterness that can lead to further conflict. Apologizing is a sign of strength, not weakness, and it is a powerful tool in preventing future conflicts in any relationship.

When to Seek Help

It is important to seek help during conflicts when the situation is becoming hostile and it appears that your daughter-in-law and you are unable to resolve the conflict on your own. If the conflict is escalating and emotions are running high, it is important to seek outside help to enable you both come up with a resolution. Professional help may be necessary if the conflict is of a serious nature. A mediator can help facilitate a productive conversation and help you both to come to a mutually beneficial agreement. Additionally, counseling may be necessary if the conflict is causing emotional distress. In any case, it is important to seek help when the conflict is too difficult to handle on your own.

CONCLUSION

Any family benefits from having a good mother-in-law. She is there to love, guide, and encourage her children as they begin new lives with their partners. She'll be the perfect bridge between the generations of mother and daughter-in-law, giving common ground for all. Any woman can become an outstanding mother-in-law who makes her son, daughters-in-law and grandchildren feel joyful and comfortable with a little effort.

The ability to appreciate her son's new home and spouse is the most vital characteristic of a positive and supportive mother-in-law. She must recognize that his new home is his and his wife's domain, and she must respect their autonomy. A good mother-in-law will also take the time to get to know her daughter-in-law, understand her struggles, and cultivate a healthy relationship with her.

It is important for a mother-in-law to show her son, daughter-in-law and grandchildren unconditional affection. She should be there to encourage them in good and difficult times and to express her gratitude for their life together. A positive mother-in-law understands that her son's marriage is not a replacement for her own relationship with him, but rather an extra bonus to his new family.

Printed in Great Britain
by Amazon

52207458R00029